c. 1950s.

KAMPONG DAYS

NATIONAL HERITAGE BOARD

*National
Archives of
Singapore*

YEARS OF ARCHIVES • THE NATION'S MEMORY BANK CELEBRATES

1968 - 1998

1, Canning Rise, Singapore, 179868, Republic of Singapore

WITH COMPLIMENTS

KAMPONG DAYS

Village Life And Times In Singapore Revisited

National Archives

c. 1960s.

Credits

The National Archives would like to acknowledge the assistance of the following persons and organisations in the production of this publication:

Chu Sui Mang; Doris Woon; Han Chou Yuan; K C Koh; Kadir Ambron; Marvin Chan; Mohamad Mustaffa; Ong Chau Ngak; Ong Ting Lye; Poh Ah Choo; Shaik Kadir; Tung Pui Hee; Quek Tiong Swee; Lianhe Zaobao; National University of Singapore Central Library; National Library; Oral History Department; Photoarchive KIT/TM; The Straits Times Press.

ADVISOR
Mrs Lily Tan

RESEARCHERS
Alison Tay; Chung Sang Hong; Irene Lim; Karthigesu Thangamma; Marian Louise de Souza; Phan Ming Yen; Sally Seah; Varughese Thomas

EDITOR
K F Tang

BOOK LAYOUT
Leah Teo

All photographs from National Archives
unless otherwise stated.

PUBLISHED BY NATIONAL ARCHIVES

140, Hill Street Building

Hill Street

Singapore 0617

Tel: 3300977/3300909

Fax: 3393583

Designed and Produced by Lancer Design Services
Block 135, Jurong East Street 13
#03-333 Singapore 2260
Tel: 562 4756 Fax: 567 7688

ISBN 9971-9908-7-3

c. 1950s.

Contents

c. 1920s.

Foreword

In today's affluent and urbanised Singapore, many young Singaporeans go to the zoo to learn about farm animals like the humble chickens, ducks, rabbits, goats and cows. They see vegetables and fruits not as fruit-bearing trees or plants but as neatly packaged in plastic bags on the shelves of air-conditioned supermarkets. Games and toys are no longer simple, self-created and home-made items using scraps of left-over wood, metal or paper. The young of today play with hi-tech computer games and battery-driven motorised toys. The slightly damaged or outdated toys are discarded and replaced by new ones. Even the present generation adult Singaporeans are no different as many of us would prefer to discard slightly damaged things than take the trouble to have them repaired. I have been told that it is cheaper thus more cost-effective to buy new things than to repair the old ones. Of course the newer model would be an improved one which can do things which the old ones cannot.

With the passing of time and many generations later, nobody would remember what life was like in the good old kampong days. Along with the disappearance of kampongs, some of the kampong values like thrift, creativity, team spirit in gotong royong, neighbourhood kinships and friendships are also very quickly forgotten. However there are of course certain not so nice aspects of kampong living which we would surely like to forget such as the secret societies/ gangs who used to terrorise the kampong dwellers and the smelly outhouse toilets. Through this book and the exhibition of photographs and artifacts, we will try to recapture not only the images, both the idyllic and the not so pretty pictures, but also the intangible, the kampong values which we hope will be retained although the physical landscape and infrastructure have changed. We hope that those who had lived in the kampongs will try and pass on to our younger generation Singaporeans our memories, the joys, the inconveniences, hardships and most importantly the kampong values of neighbourliness, thrift and hard work.

Life would be the richer if we could take with us the cultural and historical baggage of the experiences of our forefathers. Thus, wherever possible we should try and put in place, some kind of concrete reminders (like this book and exhibition) of the past for the future Singaporeans to learn and to appreciate. We, at the National Archives working on this project, are very excited and hope that the book and the exhibition would be an eye-opener for the young and a nostalgic trip down memory lane for the older and ex-kampong dwellers.

Mrs Lily Tan
Director
National Archives

c. 1960s.

Introduction

PICTURE THIS: you are travelling in the outskirts of Singapore town just over 30 years ago.

As you travel, you see people in a queue waiting to fetch water from a standpipe; or you might see children, sun-burnt and half-naked, bathing; or, more likely, just simply playing with water from the pipe.

Further beyond, you will see the many wooden houses with attap roofs where these children and people live.

If you decide to have a closer look at the houses, you will have to park your car by the roadside as the roads leading to them are narrow and not tarred.

As you walk past the wooden houses on stilts, you will hear the rustling of leaves, the clucking of chickens and the laughter of children at play.

And if it is evening, you will see the older people of the village as they sit and talk on the verandas of their houses. And after a while, you will hear the low buzz of voices … occasionally broken by laughter … from a group of youths standing in a circle and kicking a rattan ball.

But perhaps what will strike you most is the bond that seems to have been forged between the people who live in such a place.

Perhaps it was because there were few forms of indoor entertainment that the villagers had to spend more time outdoors and thus got to know one another better.

Or was it the absence of fences between the houses that made the villagers feel as if they were one?

Whatever the reasons for this, you will not really know the feeling of togetherness which comes with kampong living unless you have lived in the way the villagers lived.

The wooden houses are now gone, and some say that living in flats is different because the moment one enters one's flat, one is shut off from the rest of the world.

But then again, there are those who try to keep the "kampong spirit" alive by holding weddings in the void decks in their blocks of flats so that people can still get together like they did in the old days. And there are those who gather in void decks in the evenings just to talk, share and hold on to the memory of those days.

For if you have lived through them, kampong days never really leave you.

An early Chinese village, c. 1840s.

c. 1950s.

HISTORICAL BACKGROUND

Preface

Kampong: a Malay term for village; originally a cluster of rectangular wooden houses raised from the ground and roofed with attap, and set in gardens and rows of fruit trees; refers "normally to the most coherent social unit or community in a rural society. As a social unit, it possesses some degree of solidarity, neighbourly feeling and kinship ties. These characteristics, however, may vary from one village to another." (Source: Roziah bte Ismail, <u>Adjustment To High Rise Living</u>, Academic Exercise, Department of History, National University of Singapore, 1983.)

c. 1900s.

Kampong days go back into history *much* further than we can remember or even know. Most of us know, about kampongs from what our grandfathers and their grandfathers could remember. The kampong as we know it today had been around for 400 years.

Descriptions of what we call the "kampong" can be found in references to 14th-century Singapore. At that time, the island had been described by R. J. Wilkinson as "so much a waste land, a site for the huts of Proto-Malayan sea-gypsies".

By 1811, however, a village had been set up on the site of the old town of Singapura near the Singapore River, after the Temenggong of Johor, Temenggong Abdul Rahman, came to the island with 150 followers.

In any case, by the time Raffles arrived in Singapore in 1819, Wa Hakim, an eyewitness, reported that "At the time Tuan Raffles came, there were under 100 small houses and huts at the mouth of the river but the Raja's house was the only large one...about 30 families of Orang Laut also lived in boats a little way up the Singapore River at the wide part ... About half the Orang Laut lived ashore and half in boats. The place where the Orang Laut lived was called Kampong Temenggong."

Following the arrival of the British, immigration from nearby Indonesian islands and Peninsular Malaya gained momentum and the Malay population grew so that by the turn of the century, there were three main Malay residential areas: the first was the Kampong Glam area, which comprised a collection of Malay-style wooden houses and shops facing the Singapore River; the second was the Telok Blangah settlement, occupied mainly by the Temenggong's kinsmen and followers; and finally, Kampong Melaka, occupied by Malays from Malacca.

As Singapore flourished, Malay kampongs also developed in the rural areas. Most of the early Malay kampongs were fishing villages, and these grew along the coast and rivers. Kampongs also developed inland, and these were involved in the cultivation of coconuts and fruits.

Traditionally, however, the Malays did not settle near the city centre, where trade and commerce were the main activities. The Malays generally settled in the rural areas around the eastern coast and the interior of the island, with a relatively small concentration to the north of the Singapore River.

The Malays, however, were not the only settlers in early Singapore. According to G. W. Earl, a traveller in Singapore, "the ground at the back of the town is laid in gardens by the Chinese who grow large quantities of fruits and vegetables for the supply of the inhabitants. On the bank of the creek are many plantations of pepper and gambier, also cultivated by the Chinese." He added that the "interior of the island is almost unknown to the Europeans but there is a small independent Chinese settlement a few miles distant from the town, which is said to be very populous and as considerable quantities of produce are brought to the town for sale, their plantation must be extensive. No European has yet visited them." It is likely that some of the earliest Chinese villages came about either because of the gambier plantations located in the northern and western part of the island in the early 19th century or as farms.

An example of this would be the Nee Soon area, where most of the villages came about because of the gambier and pepper plantation and, much later, the rubber and pineapple plantations. A similar example can be found in the Jurong area, which in the 19th century was taken up primarily by

gambier plantations and by rubber plantations in the beginning of the 20th century, with estates such as Bulim Estate, Loyang Estate, Chong Keng Estate and Yunnan Estate.

At that time, vegetable and fruit farming was the main economic activity in Jurong and most of those who lived there were either farmers or plantation workers. Ang Mo Kio was another area once well known for its vegetable and fruit gardens. Other once-rural areas such as Choa Chu Kang, Yio Chu Kang and Lim Chu Kang also had their beginnings in agriculture.

Interestingly, most of the inhabitants of a particular village would be of a particular dialect group. In Jurong, for example, most villagers were Ann Kway Hokkiens while in Nee Soon, most were Hokkiens and Teochews and in Choa Chu Kang the early settlers were Teochews, although the Hokkiens later came to grow pineapples and were responsible for developing the rubber industry there. The Teochews were also prevalent in the fishing villages along the northern coast. Some of the predominantly Teochew areas included Punggol and places along the Serangoon River.

Though little known, the Eurasians too had a kampong, known as Kampong Serani in the Haig Road area. This kampong has been described as comprising 25 houses set in "three straight rows, making up three sides of a rectangle. The fourth side was sealed off by a metal fence which separated the kampong from the mansion of the owner of the kampong." Gerry Pereira, who lived there in the 1950s, wrote in his book, Singapore Eurasians: Memories and Hope, that the rent was about $20 per month for a little home of "a hall, bedroom and kitchen". This type of living continued till the Eurasian families began to move out as they upgraded their houses.

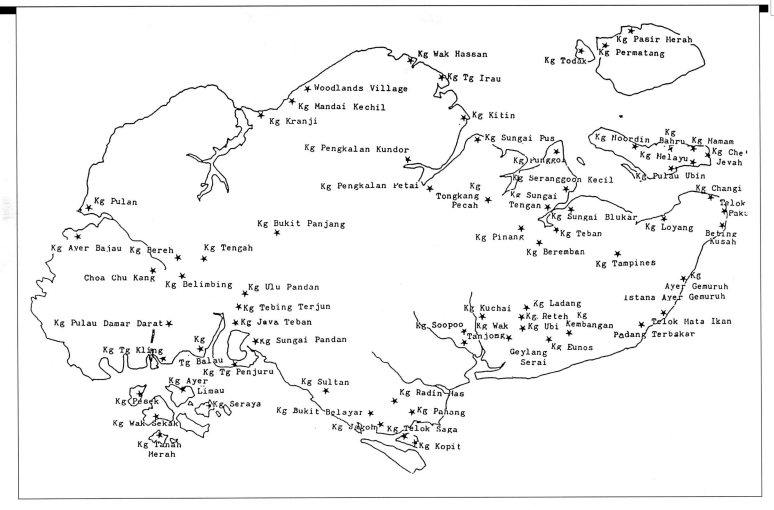

1. In the eastern part of the island, there were villages such as Kampong Siglap, Kampong Bedok, Kampong Amber, Kampong Padang Terbakar, Kampong Tamah Merah Kechil, Telok Mata Ikan, Kampong Beting Kusah and Kampong Darat Nanas. Most of these were formerly Malay fishing villages although some were involved in the cultivation of coconuts and fruit trees, as some of their names imply. Kampong Darat Nanas, for example, derived its name from the pineapple plantation that existed in the area. (Source: Kartini bte Yoyit, Vanishing Landscapes: Malay Kampongs In Singapore, Academic Exercise, Department of History, National University of Singapore 1987).

2. Malay fishing villages could also be found along the western coast of the island. Kampongs such as Kampong Tanjung Kling, Kampong Damar Barat, Kampong Tanjung Penjuru and Kampong Sungai Pandan were originally pirate hideouts masquerading as fishing villages. The original inhabitants of these villages were probably Orang Laut pirates from nearby islands. One researcher has suggested that they might have settled on the land in the 1840s because the Temenggong helped the British eliminate all piratical activities in the Singapore seas. (Source: Kartini bte Yoyit, Vanishing Landscapes: Malay Kampongs In Singapore.)

3. The four-mile stretch of Pasir Panjang beach was the site of several villages. These were established by the then new Malay immigrants and the Malays from the Temenggong's village in Telok Blangah. The immigrants were probably attracted to the area by jobs created by the new harbour while the Temenggong's followers settled there to continue fishing. The early settlers also made a living driving bullock carts in the harbour area and making and selling charcoal. (Source: Kartini bte Yoyit, Vanishing Landscapes: Malay Kampongs In Singapore.)

4. Several villages sprang up in the interior of western Singapore. Among them were Kampong Bereh, established in 1835 and located at the mouth of Sungai Bereh; Kampong Belimbing and Kampong Choa Chu Kang. (Source: Kartini bte Yoyit, Vanishing Landscapes: Malay Kampongs In Singapore.)

5. The mouths of the Serangoon, Punggol and Seletar rivers along the north-eastern coast of Singapore were also village sites. Some of the earlier kampongs were Kampong Punggol and Kampong Tongkop, by the banks of the Punggol River. One significant kampong along the northern coast was Kampong Kranji, which later became a ferry station to Johor Baru before the causeway was built in 1923. This kampong attracted many Chinese traders because it was linked to Singapore Town by Bukit Timah Road. (Source: Kartini bte Yoyit, Vanishing Landscapes: Malay Kampongs In Singapore.)

The Sembawang Rural District Committee was one of several organisations which organised floats and erected archways to celebrate the Queen Elizabeth's coronation in 1953.

c. 1960s.

RURAL BOARD

Rural Board

A Rural Board was established in 1909 to administer the rural areas, including the surrounding islands of Singapore. (The city area was administered by a Municipal Commission, which became the City Council when the title of a City was conferred by Royal Charter in 1951.) The Board consisted of the Commissioner of Lands, who acted as Chairman, the Chief Health Officer, the Director of Public Works, the Chief Surveyor and six other members nominated by the Governor. It administered directly matters such as the water supply, markets, parks and had its own building inspectorate, while health and rural engineering were administered by the government departments.

In 1947, the Board set up a number of village committees to foster contacts with

Accompanied by Che Awang, Penghulu of Punggol Village, Mr Lim Siew Ek, Chairman of the Serangoon Rural District Committee, Dr A Thevathasen, President of the Rotary Club and Sir William Goode, the last Governor of Singapore, toured the kampong in 1955

the people in the rural areas. The village committees acted as liaison bodies and in an advisory capacity between the villagers and the Board. By organising regular meetings, the committees helped to ascertain the needs of the rural public, such as improved health

conditions, sanitation, buildings, water and agricultural requirements, child welfare, and recreation and cultural facilities. The committees were able to put forward suggestions to the Board to provide for these needs.

Eventually, the village committees became seven Rural District Committees, namely, Bukit Panjang Rural District Committee, Sembawang Rural District Committee, Serangoon Rural District Committee, Changi Rural District Committee, Bedok Rural District Committee, Pasir Panjang Rural District Committee and Bukit Timah Rural District Committee.

The Rural District Committees had no statutory powers or direct representation on the Rural Board. Members, who were initially nominated by the Board, were subsequently elected. The tenure of office for committee members was one year.

The committees worked to improve rural life. They asked for standpipes and water supplies in areas where water was scarce or unsafe for drinking; for electricity; for maternity and child welfare services; for schools, transport services and better market and postal facilities; for recreation grounds; for names to be given to unnamed villages; for open-air film shows; for help and guidance in the building of low-cost houses; for traffic safety measures and an adequate police service. The Rural District Committees were an integral part of the average rural dweller's life.

In 1953, membership of the Rural Board was enlarged from 10 to 18 to include representatives from each of the seven Rural District Committees. This was done to increase the participation of the rural population in local government affairs so that the true interests of rural dwellers could be properly looked after.

Under the Local Government Ordinance of 1957, a provision was made to establish three District Councils; namely, Katong, Serangoon and Jurong/Bukit Panjang to replace the Rural Board. Each District Council was to consist of a Chairman appointed by the Governor, 12 elected members and three nominated members. With the establishment of the Katong, Serangoon and Jurong/Bukit Panjang District Councils on 1 September 1958, more attention was

given to the respective districts, and consequently, increased amenities were provided in the rural areas. The seven Rural District Committees also stepped up their activities in looking after the welfare of the rural population.

The Rural Board's staff was decentralised and the offices of the Katong, Serangoon and Jurong/Bukit Panjang District Councils started functioning from 1 September 1958. All transactions with the Rural Board were then made at these centres. The main office of the Board was, however, maintained by a skeleton staff.

Mr Lim Nee Soon and his son, Lim Chong Pang, served on the Rural Board from 1913 to 1921 and 1929 to 1938 respectively.

A river kampong in Pulau Sumulun, c. 1950s.

c. 1960s.

c. 1950s.

THE KAMPONG HOUSE

Preface

While one might think of the rural house as merely an ensemble of wooden planks with zinc sheets or attap draped over as a roof without much thought or detailed planning, a closer look at the kampong house reveals an architectural form which portrays the historical, cultural and religious backgrounds of the villagers and their interaction with the environment ...

Ten "Easy" Steps To Building
A Traditional Malay House

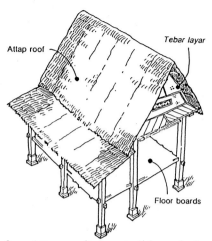

9. Attap roofing material, made from thatch, is sewn onto a spine. The attap is then sewn overlapping each other onto the kasau attap. Floor boards and the tebar layer are also laid.

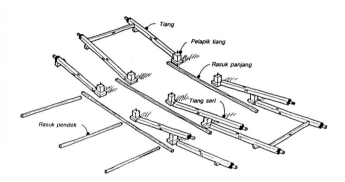

1. The site is cleared and footings and structural components laid in position.

10. The walls, windo[ws] are made and fi[...] house.

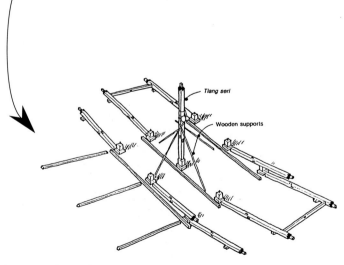

2. The tiang seri, after being erected with a pulley and the help of other villagers, is braced with wooden supports.

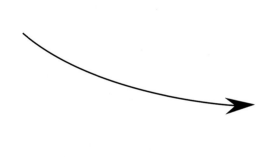

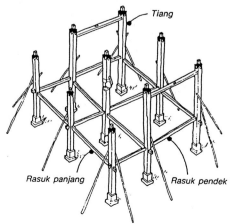

3. Other columns are erected and braced by the floor joists, crossbars and wooden supports.

4. A tem[porary] facili[...]

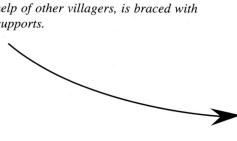

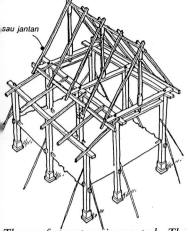

...sau jantan

The roof structure is erected. The kasau jantan (principal rafters) support the kasau lintang (purlins) which in turn support the kasau attap (common rafters).

I help build your house You help build mine, c. 1950s.

Building a house was often done in <u>gotong royong</u> style. Usually, all the villagers helped in the activity and everyone took turns to build each other's house. The houses were made of timber, had attap or zinc roofs and were lit by kerosene lamps.

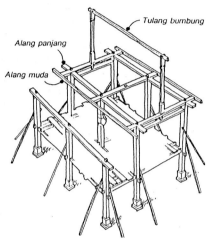

Tulang bumbung

Alang panjang

Alang muda

7. The tulang bumbung (roof ridge) is erected, supported by the king posts. The alang panjang or the serambi and the alang muda are also put up.

...dows

...her panels ...plete the

...r is made to ...ction of the roof.

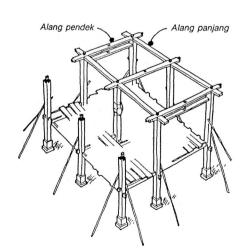

Alang pendek   Alang panjang

5. The alang panjang (girts) and the alang pendek (tie-girts) are erected.

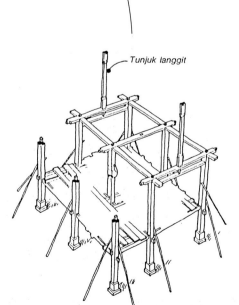

Tunjuk langgit

6. The tunjut langgit (king posts) are erected and braced by crossbars.

Source: Lim Jee Yuan, <u>The Malay House: Rediscovering Malaysia's Indigenous Shelter System</u>, Institut Masyarakat, 1987.

The Malay Kampong House

Attap (thatch) was the traditional material for the roof of the kampong house. Common types of attap were derived from the <u>nipah</u> palm, <u>rumbia</u> and <u>bertam</u>.

Zinc roofs were introduced in the 1930s but their use declined during the Second World War. Zinc was then highly priced and many villagers sold their metal roofs to the Japanese and went back to attap roofs. After the war, however, zinc roofs returned.

At the entrance to Malay kampong houses, the stairs led to a covered porch know as the <u>anjung</u>. <u>Anjungs</u> were favourite places to rest and chat. Chairs and benches were often found along the sides of the porch. More basic houses, however, either did not have <u>anjungs</u>, or only very small ones.

Malay kampong houses were traditionally built on stilts or pillars. The raised level enabled the house to escape damage by floods and tidewater, avoid intrusions by animals and catch the cooling wind. Besides, the family could enjoy more privacy and have extra space under the house for the storage of fuel (firewood, coconut leaves), farming implements, bicycles and other items.

Coconut trees often formed part of the scenic beauty of kampongs, especially those near a river or the sea. The trees were important to kampong dwellers because various parts of them were used for fuel, making implements, construction and food.

The typical Malay kampong house consisted of three main areas: the <u>ibu rumah</u> (main room), the <u>ruang tamu</u> (reception room) and the <u>dapur</u> (kitchen).

The <u>ibu rumah</u> was the core of the house. It was the largest room in the house and usually located on the highest level. Many activities, like praying, studying, sleeping, ironing, and even feasting, took place in this room.

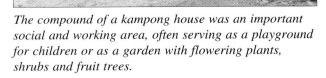

The compound of a kampong house was an important social and working area, often serving as a playground for children or as a garden with flowering plants, shrubs and fruit trees.

The <u>dapur</u> was important for women, not so much as a place for cooking and cleaning, but as a social area. As traditional Malay customs required the segregation of men and women in certain social situations, women often used different rooms from men. The men were usually in the front of the house (the <u>ruang tamu</u> or the <u>ibu rumah</u>) while the women were in or around the kitchen, which was situated at the back of the house and usually at the lowest level.

The Chinese Kampong House

Rural Chinese houses were usually rectangular or square and built on earthen platforms, or sometimes on cement of brick foundations. The houses were usually built to face south because in Chinese geomancy, the south represents good luck and the north and west bad luck.

A distinctive feature of the rural Chinese house was the inscribed board above the main door. The inscription told which part of China the house-owner's ancestors came from and revealed the names of the family hall too. The board was usually rectangular and painted red and the Chinese characters were either in black or gold.

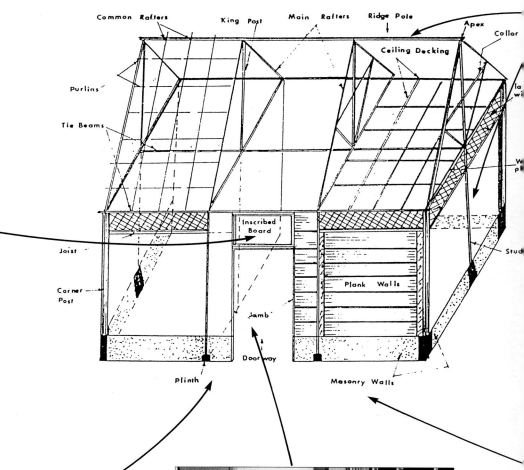

Chinese kampong houses sometimes had a set of words attached to each side of the front door. Called <u>dui lian</u>, (对联), these words were proverb-like sayings in verse.

Just as the <u>ibu rumah</u> was the most important room in the Malay kampong house, the living room was also the most important in the Chinese house. The room was usually centrally located for easy access to all occupants and most family activities and gatherings took place there.

Rural Chinese houses often had window bars for security. The bars were either vertical or horizontal and their number was always five or seven, so that the spacing between them provided both security and allowed for ventilation at the same time.

Basic Layouts Of
Chinese Rural Houses

Collection of Han Chou Yuan, courtesy of National Archives.

Kitchens in Chinese kampong houses were often shared by more than one family. For example, the newly-wedded children, living in a different compound, shared the use of their parents' kitchen.

RECTANGULAR HOUSE PLAN

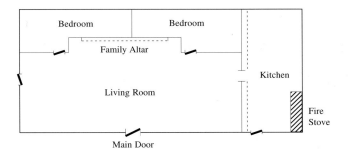

Scale : 1 : 300 Cm

The compound of the house was also the children's playground. The open space outside the house was also frequently used for a leisurely chat, as indicated by the presence of chairs and benches outside. The entrance is abstructed so the main door could be kept open. The half-gate enabled mothers busy with housework to keep their young children indoors while keeping inquisitive chickens and ducks outside the house as well!

SQUARE HOUSE PLAN

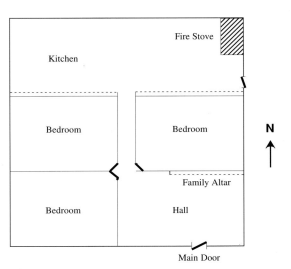

Scale : 1 : 300 Cm

Source: Toh Meng Soon, <u>A Geographical Study of Rural Chinese Houses in Singapore, 1945 - 1980.</u> Academic Exercise, Department of History, National University of Singapore, 1981.

c. 1960s.

c. 1960s.

KAMPONG LIFE

Seen Through The Eyes Of A Child

Preface

You would not see or hear this now: the wild abandon of children leaping into the river for a bath or swim; the excited chatter of boys looking for grasshoppers and spiders among the bushes; and the ingenuity with which children created their own toys.

Perhaps it was the open space or perhaps it was just that there were few forms of entertainment or that schooling seemed less pressurised that made growing up in the village take on the feeling you get when you watch a kite drift so freely in the evening sky...

Kampong Games

The all-familiar capteh, a game of Malay origin, was a kampong favourite, c. 1970s. The capteh had a rubber base pierced by a nail, to which chicken feathers were fastened. The players kicked the capteh to keep it in the air, scoring a point for each successful kick.

Children having fun with a tube, c. 1970s.

Deriving much fun from a make-shift game of tin milk cans and strings, c. 1970s.

"Life was very carefree in those days. For a boy of, maybe, say, 10 to 12 years, life was all play. We were just drifting along like a kite in the sky," reminisced Mr Shaik Kadir, who spent his childhood in the kampongs at Geylang Serai. "And some of the places we went to or some of the things we did are not found today, like vegetable farms, caves, shooting water-birds with catapults and making guns out of wood," said the 46-year-old publications editor with the Institute of Technical Education.

"Kampong life for us boys was all play and play", he further recollected," My activities on a typical Sunday would be as follows:

7.30 am I would wake up and then bath with the water I had brought back from the standpipe the day before. The water was kept in a kerosene drum in the kitchen, which was actually just a small enclosure behind the house.

8.00 am Breakfast consisted of bread which we would eat with curry left over from the night before or with some kaya which my mother had bought from the provision shop. I would take my breakfast together with my mother and two younger sisters. Sometimes, we would eat putu mayam which we bought from an Indian man who went around on a bicycle.

8.30 am After breakfast, I was all ready to play. I would look for my friends, who would in turn also be looking for other friends. There would be about six of us at most. If there was too large a group, we would have difficulty making decisions, but if there were too few of us, we would be in trouble if we met up with other boys when we passed other kampongs.

9 am – 2 pm One favourite place was a cave which was beyond the vegetable farms. We went there because the cave was eerie There were bats in it. It was fun going there ... like an adventure. There were lots of swamps and marshes to cross and at the ponds, we would shoot water-birds with our catapults. They could be eaten and if we were lucky, we would be able to get three or four. Best of all, if there were sharpshooters among us, we could get up to 10 birds and we would divide the birds among us to take home to be cooked. We would carry the birds along with us to the cave, which was about four to five kilometres beyond the farmland. There, we would disturb the bats and eat the fruits from the trees that grew there. There were mango trees, guava trees, and all sorts of other fruit trees. When we were hungry and tired, we would go home. That would be around 1 or 2 pm. We would take another route back.

2.00 pm Lunch would consist of rice, ikan bilis, salted egg or salted fish. It was very simple food and it was cheap but it tasted good.

5.00 pm We played games in the evening. We played catching or cowboys and Indians. Sometimes we played games with capte and tops. We also flew kites during the kite-flying season. We made many of our own toys. Things like capte were made from nails and pieces of rubber

The Blind Man's Buff was another favourite game, c. 1960s.

and feathers which we plucked from roosters. The guns which we used were made from pieces of wood we found lying about. The catapult was made from wood from the 'Y' twigs of the tembusu tree.

8.00 pm In the night, there was nothing to do. I would be asleep by 8 or 9 pm and, as far as I know, by 10 pm, most people in the kampong would be asleep. Of course there were old wives' tales and superstitions about ghosts and pontianaks. At night, the kampongs were dark and quiet, and you could hear the owls. This made it more scary to play in the kampong after 8 pm".

Like Mr Shaik, Madam Poh Ah Choo, 50, who grew up in Henderson Village, also recalled a fear of the dark and the supernatural.

"It was scary as the kampong then was so dark. We only had oil lamps then," she said. "When we went for wayang, we would be so frightened after the show was over we would run home as fast as we could. It was really dark but we all knew the route well and just dashed straight home. We were afraid of ghosts … people used to tell us not to go out in the night because they often heard strange noises."

As for her own scary experiences, she said: "When I was a little older, I had to fetch water from the public tap and sometimes I had to wait until 2 am. There were times when I saw people bathing under a tree from afar but when I got closer, there was no one! There were also strange noises in the kampong and many old people

knew how to listen to these. They said it was the ghosts. You could hear them very often in the kampong. I feel scared now as I tell you."

However, this fear of the dark and the supernatural was but one aspect of a more idyllic and carefree childhood.

"Children were naughtier in the kampong. There were so many games to play, like climbing trees, ball games, catching fish and the like. When it rained, it was a good time to catch fish. Yes, I was very happy," recounted the housewife, who now lives in Hougang.

"We made our own kites, and that cost us nothing. We just got some sticks from the brooms and used some glue to stick the paper on it, that's all. And when I was not at school, I helped my mother rear pigs and cook pig feed", added Madam Poh, who lived with her parents, grandmother and seven siblings in the kampong. Her father was a pig-farmer who also sold <u>dou-gan</u> (豆干).

But she also recalled less-than-comfortable living conditions, unlike those which come with modern living in flats.

"We had to walk for about an hour to get to the bus-stop. We rarely went out, but there were hawkers who came around to sell things. Also, there was not much need for refrigerators for we had no money to buy expensive food like fish all the time. We had to share all our food. For instance, when we had an orange, it would be split into four parts and all our us would eat one slice real slowly."

Catching fish in the monsoon drain or <u>longkang</u> was one of the fun activities of the kampong kids, c. 1970s. Others included climbing <u>buah cherry</u> trees and spider hunting.

An evergreen among girls, <u>five stones</u> is played by two or more players individually using five small triangular cloth bags filled with rice, sand or saga seeds, c. 1970s. The object is to score points by completing a set pattern of play.

The <u>layang-layang</u> or kite has always fascinated children, c. 1960s. The kites were made from light bamboo strips and thin, oily, water-proof paper or cellophane. Some children coated the strings of their kites with pulverised glass for "fighting" with other kites in the sky. The <u>layang-layang</u> is still seen in Singapore skies.

The <u>goli panjang</u> or marble game is played by two or more players each aiming to collect as many marbles as possible, c. 1970s.

Kampong schoolchildren studied in a humble environment with limited facilities, c. 1960s.

Due to inadequate space, some classes of Kay Wah School were conducted on this borrowed wayang stage, c. 1970s. Very often, two classes separated by a wooden board were on simultaneously.

Education

c. 1960s.

Yet, the life of a kampong child was not just play, play and play. The kampongs were not short of schools for most villagers knew the importance of education and had built their own schools.

"The schools were built by the kampong people ... the richer ones. They would then look for their own teachers. I think education was free for all. The richer parents would also donate some money," said Madam Poh.

But while most, if not all, children go to school these days, this was not so with the children of the past. And so it was with the kampong children too.

Mr Shaik recalled: "As I remember, very few of us went to school. I had friends who never went to school. Perhaps only half of them did and even then, it was quite common for many of them to drop out from school when they failed in their exams to get into secondary school."

Similarly, Madam Poh noted: "Very few children went to school. Parents were not very strict about education and many boys played truant. It was very different from the present. Also, many people said that girls didn't need education."

Mr Ong Chau Ngak, who lived in a village in Lim Chu Kang, shed a different light on why some villagers were less serious about education.

"In the old days, my grandfather didn't think education was important. As long as his children could understand a few words and could write their names, he was happy."

Mr Ong thought that this could possibly be because they lived on a farm and did not depend on formal education for their livelihood.

"My father was more open-minded and he would like his children to study as much as their capability allowed. However, our circumstances did not allow. The farm kept us very busy as we didn't employ any helpers from outside. Therefore, we couldn't pursue our studies very far," added Mr Ong, whose family owned a pig farm.

However, school did play a part in the life of a child growing up in a kampong. In fact, a glance at the syllabuses for the kampong school reveals that they allowed the child growing up in rural areas to learn about life outside the village.

Said Madam Tung Pui Hee, who attended Chuen Min School in the Bukit Ho Swee area from 1953 to 1958: "We studied subjects like History, English, Maths, Good Citizen, General Knowledge."

For those who grew up in the kampongs, school would always be part of their fond memories, whether as a place where they could meet more friends or where the village kid could learn about the world beyond his immediate kampong. And for those who did not have the opportunity, schooling was something which was greatly desired.

Said Madam Poh: "My elder sister was not educated but my younger sister was. Every time I see my sister carrying her bag to school, I would be so envious and thought to myself how wonderful it would be if I could go too."

c. 1960s.

Old-fashioned writing schools (si shu (私塾)) for the Chinese and religious Quran schools for the Malays marked the beginning of education in rural Singapore. The British colonial government paid close attention to the education of Malays but adopted a laissez-faire attitude towards education for the Chinese and Indian communities. Before the war, kampong Chinese si shu (私塾) were mostly set up by clan or dialect associations, membership of which was the only requirement for admission to the schools. A class was usually formed by 20 to 30 children of varying ages. An "old-style" curriculum which included teaching the Four Books and Five Classics was imparted. The schools remained common in rural areas even in the 1930s. Modern Chinese schools were introduced in the early 1920s because of the developing political and literary movements in China. In kampong areas, these schools were attended mostly by boys, and some girls from rich families. After the war, enrolment in schools all over Singapore expanded as many school-children and teenagers resumed their war-disrupted education.

The enrolment in kampong schools peaked in the late 1950s and early 1960s as more post-war babies came of age. During this period, the total primary school enrolment was 313,294, making up 84.1 per cent of the total school population. Of the 445 primary schools in Singapore, half, or 224, were in the rural areas. Among these rural schools,

133 were Chinese schools
(49 per cent of all Chinese schools)

53 were English schools
(35 per cent of all English schools)

32 were Malay schools
(71 per cent of all Malay schools)

6 were Tamil schools
(40 per cent of all Tamil schools)

From the mid-1970s, more parents preferred to send their children to English-medium schools, which were mainly in urban areas, and kampong schools faced declining enrolments.

In the 1980s, the language medium for all schools was standardised, with English as the first language and the mother tongue as the second language. Also, many kampongs were demolished to make way for new housing estates and their residents resettled. Kampong school population thus declined and many kampong schools were either closed down or moved to HDB estates.

A Day In The Life of
Kampong Schoolchildren

Most kampong kids went to school on foot or by bicycle as the schools were usually within walking distance of their homes, c. 1950s.

A kampong school was typically a single-storey building of timber or cement with a corrugated iron roof. Photo shows Pei Hsin Public School, off 26 km Chua Chu Kang Road, c. 1960s.

Normally, pupils came in as early as 7.30 am to attend the flag-raising ceremony followed by morning exercise. Photo shows a morning assembly at Sin Ming Primary School, c. 1960s.

Collection of Marvin Chan, courtesy of National Archives.

A post-war Malay language textbook cover depicted girls and boys as having equal opportunities to receive an education.

Education for Malay girls received a boost under Windstedt's administration. (In 1916, R. O. Windstedt was Director of Education of the Colony and the Federated Malay States.) Realising the educational plight of Malay girls, Windstedt appointed a qualified Lady Supervisor of Malay Girls' School. In 1925, he appointed an Assistant Supervisor for Malay Education to promote equal education opportunities for both sexes.

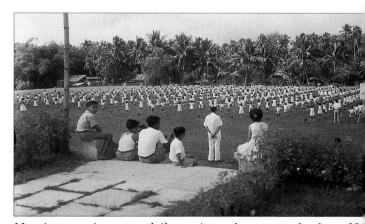

Morning exercise was a daily routine at kampong schools, c. 196

Collection of Marvin Chan, courtesy of National Archives.

Collection of Marvin Chan, courtesy of National Archives.

Bookcovers of some children's reading materials in the 1950s. Many of these were imported from Hong Kong and China. Later, because of the colonial government's efforts to standardise and "Malayanise" the syllabus of different language streams, locally-published children's books filled the shelves of school libraries and bookshops.

In the post-war period, most schools in Singapore had half-day sessions, from 8 am to 1 pm. Afternoon sessions were also conducted in many primary school buildings, c. 1960s.

A Day In The Life of Kampong Schoolchildren

In-between lessons, there was usually a 10-minute break when pupils could enjoy a quick snack or some fun and games, c. 1960s.

Many kampong schools were closed down in the early 198... enrolment. The picture above shows pupils of Pei Hsin Pu... PSLE. At the end of 1982, the 30-year-old school, which ... closed for good.

Students were given free skimmed milk during recess under a school feeding scheme for under-nourished children, c. 1950s.

Answering calls of nature was easier said than done when the entire school had only one dilapidated, cramped and stinking toilet, c. 1960s. In many kampong schools, there was no differentiation between the boys' and the girls' toilets.

On certain days, mass tooth-brushing was compulsory during recess, c. 1970s.

For all their schools' humble environment and limited facilities, school life was memorable for kampong children. What they had was space to run about in and for other outdoor activities.

c.1970s.

Extra-curricular activities in kampong schools were oriented towards the schoolchildren's environment and helped the students to gain practical skills and to develop stronger bonds with their school and community

c.1970s.

of dwindling
sitting for their
pupils that year,

A Graduation Ceremony... and with that, school life ended for another batch of primary six pupils, c. 1960s. After receiving their school leaving certificates, many kampong children started working to support themselves and their families. Very few had the privilege of a secondary education. In the early 1960s, total secondary school enrolment was 59,458, or 16 per cent of the total school population. Fewer than four in ten of the 74 secondary schools then existing were in rural areas. Kampong children who made the grade aimed to go to the urban secondary schools because these had higher academic standards and better facilities.

c.1970s.

No cars or buses after school... These Hua Mien School pupils, like most kampong schoolchildren, walked or cycled home, c. 1960s.

c.1970s.

c. 1960s.

c. 1950s.

KAMPONG LIFE

Seen Through The Eyes Of A Housewife

Preface

While the kampong child's life might have revolved around fun and play, the housewife's concerns were more mundane and routine and in some ways not unlike those of a present-day housewife. Except that for the kampong housewife, memories of kampong days include having to cook without the convenience of gas or electricity, or taps in the house to provide water...

Kampong Festivities

c. 1960s.

c. 1970s.

"It was a very joyous occasion when people get married in the kampong," recalled Madam Poh of her wedding when she was 21 years old.

"Many people would crowd round to watch. At that time, everybody wanted to see the bride putting on make-up. Tents would be set up in the front part of the bride's house. During the day, the bride's friends and relatives would come and in the night, the groom's friends and relatives would be there."

Madam Poh also said that invitation cards were delivered personally, unlike today, when cards are passed through friends or sent by mail.

"If some guests were not invited, they would ask friends and relatives to invite them personally on the day of the wedding."

On the wedding day itself, the matchmaker would take the bride to the groom's house. According to Madam Poh, when the bride got into the groom's car, it was a common practice for the groom to bang the door loudly so that she would get a shock and be submissive to him in the future. The bride was also not allowed to lift her head.

c. 1960s.

c. 1960s.

c. 1960s.

Malay Wedding

Kampong festivities were generally not confined to the family. Everyone in the village pitched in. The spirit of togetherness was most evident at kampong weddings — particularly Malay weddings. If a big pot was needed, one villager would lend the pot. Someone else would set up the tent — and so on. The spirit of <u>gotong royong</u> ran high on such occasions.

A tent was usually put up in the courtyard next to the house and able and willing hands rendered help, c. 1970s. Preparations included laying the long table where food was placed.

Men dishing out from huge cauldrons, the food for the <u>kenduri</u> (feast), c. 1970s.

c. 1970s.

She recalled: "It was quite a frightening experience to be a bride then. The groom then seemed to be very fierce. But it was all very funny. It was all done in good spirit. When the bride arrived, you could hear everyone shouting, 'Here comes the bride, come and see the bride'."

After the wedding, Madam Poh lived with her in-laws, who owned a joss stick shop. "I was not allowed to do anything. I just watched over the house and answered the calls."

But Madam Poh did have to do her share of shopping and cooking.

"I did my marketing at Redhill market, which was about 20 minutes away from home. Things were cheap then. We had 10 people in the family and with $5 there was still money left over after marketing. We had many helpers and so, as a cook, you must think of different things to cook every day or else people will start to ask: 'Aren't you sick of eating the same dish?'

"The most popular dish then was sweet potato leaf or "huan tzi heo". And there was no rice cooker, so we had to use wood or kerosene stoves. Also, there was no electricity and there were public taps for water. It was too expensive to install a tap in the house."

c. 1960s.

'970s.

c. 1960s.

c. 1960s.

...eaking for a communal-styled lunch in the midst ...the activity, c, 1970s. It was on such occasions ...t the young men and women of the kampong got ...know other young men and women from other ...mpongs. Lasting relationships started this way!

The performing Malay band, a regular feature at Malay weddings and celebrations, c. 1970s.

Bride, with head bowed as a gesture of respect, c. 1970s.

Worship

Kampong residents were free to practise their own faith and it was not uncommon to find a temple and a surau (mosque) within a kampong. There was religious harmony among the villagers. The Malays would go to the surau, the Chinese, the village temples and the Christians, the churches of different denominations. The Indians celebrated their festivals in their local village Hindu temples.

A group of Malay children celebrating Hari Raya Puasa, c. 1930s.

Masjid Bedok Laut, c. 1970s.

One of the first things the Malays would do after setting up house in the kampong was to build a surau. The villagers usually made monthly contributions towards the building of the surau. Besides being a place of worship, the surau also served as a communication centre. After evening prayers, the villagers would stay behind and chat for a while. Important activities like meetings were held here and each month, films would be screened.

Muslims going for prayers at the surau, dressed in their traditional Hari Raya best, c. 1970s.

For traditionally Malay kampongs like Kampong Siglap, the cemetery would be near, just behind the houses, c. 1970s.

During the month of Ramadan, from about the 20th night onwards, the kampong houses would be lit up with oil lamps. The womenfolk would prepare cakes, sweetmeats and great varieties of food for the New Year celebrations.

On the first day of Hari Raya, the villagers would visit their relatives and friends. At all the homes visited, there was much to eat. Children especially enjoyed themselves eating and playing. The adults would go to pray at the nearby surau.

Celebrated in January or February, Thaipusam is a celebration of the victory of good over evil, c. 1960s. Devotees carry kavadis after the vows they had made have been fulfilled. The villagers celebrated in their own village temples.

The Sree Balasubramaniam Temple in Sembawang, 1993. This is one of several smaller Hindu temples located in the outskirts of Singapore. Most of these have been or are being relocated to make way for redevelopment.

Most early Chinese immigrants were from Fujian (福建) or Guangdong (广东) province and those from the same dialect groups formed associations to look after the welfare of their community, set up schools and settled communal disputes. Some pioneers also contributed to the building of temples. Temple architecture was varied, with some temples following the style of their parent temples in China. Like the surau, the Chinese temple also served as a meeting place for villagers who gathered for important discussions, or just for tea or a game of Chinese chess. Those who were ill could go there to seek blessings and healing.

The small shack with an altar was one of the many small temples found in the villages, c. 1970s. Once the villagers believed that a spirit resided in a tree or a particular spot, an altar with offerings to the deity would be put up there, in the hope that the deity would protect them and bring them luck.

This temple in Somapah Bedok Village was dedicated to Da Ba Gong (大伯公), represented as a happy-looking, white bearded old man, c. 1970s. Sailors prayed to him for safe voyages.

The Chinese Christian Church in Nee Soon was established as early as 1909 and its supporters included Teo Eng Hock and Lim Nee Soon. In 1924, the church was relocated to a site near Jalan Ulu Seletar to make way for the expansion of Thong Aik Rubber Factory. The land for the new church was donated by Lim Nee Soon, who also contributed towards its construction.

In the 1960s, the church building deteriorated and had to be renovated. The renovation was completed in 1967.

Children playing with water from a standpipe in Geylang Serai, c. 1960s.

Village Amenities

c. 1970s.

The lack of amenities mentioned by Madam Poh was a common theme which cropped up in conversations with those who had lived in the kampongs.

Mr Ismail bin Hassan, who lived in Kampong Jalan Mata Ayer from 1958 till 1983 when the kampong was resettled, said in an oral history interview about the absence of such amenities: "The kampong people, they try to survey if there is any stream or water or what to do next. Either we have to dig wells or what. Then before that, we tried to survey the nearby stream and accidentally found a stream like a lake. So we got water from there."

He also recalled that there were three hot wells in the area of a nearby factory and that that there was also spring water which the villagers used for bathing and washing.

As for drinking water, he said that the villagers dug wells. "With the co-operation of the spirit of _gotong-royong_, we managed to build the first and then other wells. The wells were more than 20 feet deep. We managed to build 10 wells before the piped water supply came."

However, obtaining drinking water from wells presented its own problems.

"It was hard digging the wells. Sometimes we try to dig, reach down to the bottom, still we cannot get water. All muddy. So, we try to distill the water. Until the mud goes down, then we take the water and boil it. The wells ran dry during the dry season."

Water Supply

Although Singapore had an excellent water supply by the 1950s and the provision of a safe water supply was regarded by the authorities as one of the most important public health measures, only a limited number of residents benefitted.

In gazetted villages, piped water, which was under the control of the Municipal Health Department, was available to individual households. But because many villagers could not afford piped water, the Rural Board erected public standpipes wherever possible at the earliest opportunity to provide kampong communities with potable water. In 1955, 56 standpipes were installed by the Board. But in the most remote areas, well water was still important.

Most wells were built indoors beside the kitchen. Well water was used for cooking, washing and bathing. Wells were also found outdoors, usually in front of bathrooms. The water drawn from these would be conveyed through a trough to a container in the bathroom.

During the dry weather each year, the Rural Board had to supply drinking water to several areas on the mainland by water wagon, and to the offshore islands by boat, c. 1959. Shallow wells formed the chief source of water supply and they tended to dry up during droughts. In some small islands, there was no suitable water-holding stratum and well water was brackish. Rainwater could not be stored as the roofs of the houses were permeable.

A public standpipe in Toa Payoh village, c. 1960s.

Where drains had been constructed to combat malaria, "anti-malarial" wells provided a relatively safe water supply. Twenty-four such wells were built in 1955. Picture shows an anti-malarial washing well, 1951.

c. 1970s.

As for the cooking facilities, Buang bin Hj Siraj, who lived in Kampong Pasiran, recalled the use of firewood. "For cooking, we had to get wood from the rubber estate at the back...the small, small pieces and then bring them back. Other than wood, we used water for cooking, nothing else...charcoal was considered very expensive so no one burning charcoal for cooking...they only used charcoal when there was a festival, like wedding or circumcision ceremony."

Electricity too was uncommon in the kampongs.

Recalled Mr Ismail: "We used kerosene lamps. The kerosene pump, you know, the 'Butterfly' brand. Sometimes, we used candle. When something happens — candle, as a last resort. As long as it could be seen at night, just to prevent intruders or what, we were happy. But the minimum we actually had was a kerosene lamp."

Much later, however, electricity was supplied to the kampong from a generator in Sembawang. "We contracted a contractor. So we paid contributions monthly. I think monthly about $2 each per house. We contributed as a whole and paid the contractor. Only 15 years after we moved did we have electricity supply installed by the government."

c. 1970s.

c. 1970s.

Public Health

Besides the water supply, the Rural Board was also concerned with other public services like sewage disposal, public cleansing and conservancy and malaria control in the rural areas. These services were administered jointly with government departments.

c. 1960s.

Refuse disposal was by incineration, controlled tipping or composting, c. 1960s. The authorities provided collecting stations in the rural areas in addition to subsidiary collecting points in the villages. The refuse was taken to the collecting station by handcart and from there to the disposal point by contractors' lorries.

In the days before the water-borne system of sewage disposal, night-soil in the rural areas was disposed of either by the bucket system, by septic tanks or by bored-hole open latrines, c. 1960s.

Mosquito control was covered by a centrally-administered mosquito squad which visited all parts of the rural areas to check constantly on all potential breeding places of dangerous mosquitoes, 1955. The squad also carried out special surveys.

Residual spraying with DDT inside a house, 1955.

A travelling dispensary, c. 1950s.

Health Facilities

Aside from the daily routine of shopping, cooking and housekeeping, the health of her children was also one of Madam Poh's concerns.

Nowadays, our immediate reaction to someone falling ill would be to see a doctor. This was not always the case for those who lived in villages. According to Madam Poh, the villagers rarely fell ill, or when they did, they sought the help of deities or local physicians.

She recalled: "We didn't go to the doctor. Most of the time, we went and sought the deities. If that did not work, we would go and get a doctor. But it was so difficult because you needed a car to fetch the doctor. We had to go so far to fetch a car and spend some 100 dollars, which is equivalent to 1,000 dollars now. Otherwise, we would ask the Chinese physician."

It was not uncommon those days for villagers to have more faith in their own physicians or "bomohs".

"Old people, they afraid of the doctor because they never see them and trust them, last time not many doctors, unlike today. Last time, people afraid of 'orang putih' (the white man), if they see orang putih, they called all the children to hide in the house some sort like they see a tiger. They trust the bomoh. For them, if the bomoh cannot treat them, then die, 'dielah'," said Mr Awang Osman, who was born and lived in a village in Punggol, till he moved to an HDB flat in the late 1980s.

A similar observation on the villagers' fear of doctors was made by Mr Yusof Kassim, who lived in Pulau Tekong and moved to an HDB flat in the mid-80s. "Last time they never trust doctor, scared of doctor and hospital. A clinic was started there in 1949, Malay midwife, made own napkin, bought white cloth, cut and sew, 12 cents or 13 cents per yard. After a lot of people cured after receiving doctor treatment, they began to trust doctor."

If there was one disease that the villagers were afraid of, it was smallpox.

"Villagers were afraid of smallpox. Nobody knew how to cure this, they were afraid of being detained for quarantine because this disease could spread to the other members of the family and other people, therefore orang putih will catch and quarantine them at home or send them to Pulau Sekijang. Villagers flocked to see them (nurse or doctor to give vaccination). They frightened because after getting the vaccination they got fever and smallpox...like corn seed everywhere on the body, face. After the officer left, the villagers came back."

An interesting observation of health conditions in rural Singapore and of the travelling dispensaries can be found in an account by Perumal Saravana, who worked with the travelling dispensaries in the late 1950s.

He said: "There were three large vans equipped with mixtures, tablets and dressing equipment and I'm asked to take charge of the travelling dispensary with a driver and an attendant. And under my supervision, they carry on the work of dispensing and getting the particulars of the patients in the kampong area."

He added that the vans operated in various parts of the island. "Those days, there were lots of kampongs, no flats and sometimes, the kampongs write to the government requesting for vans so a person will go and inspect the place. The common types of illnesses

that we tended to were fever, gastric, pain, cough, cold, rashes and septic sores. Those days, the hygiene was very bad in the kampong areas, No proper sanitation so that there were lots of septic sores."

c. 1960s.

c. 1960s.

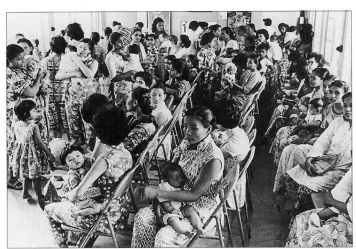

c. 1960s.

Maternal And Child Welfare

Maternal and Child and Infant Welfare Services started in 1909, at first in the urban area. A service for the care of mothers and infants in the rural area was started in 1927 with the recruitment of a Public Health Matron. Faith in western medicine was mainly confined to the educated classes but even amongst these, it was the more daring who would defy local custom and prejudice. The Malay bidan, the bomoh, the dukun, the Chinese sinseh, and the Indian ayurvedic and Unani physicians laid heavy claims in those days on the credulity of a people long accustomed to the influence of supernatural agencies with which only the local medicine man could by devious means successfully contend.

The infant service had therefore to contend with numerous adverse and curious customs and rites to which the ailing mother and the crying infant had to be subjected. As even the most optimistic then had doubts about the effectiveness of the infant service for a long time to come, nothing ambitious or comprehensive was contemplated and the Public Health Matron was merely asked to start a service as she thought flt. A small nursing staff was assembled and informal clinic sessions were started and held at irregular intervals. The initial response was cool until a little later when the nursing staff started to visit the homes of mothers. From 1929, the trickle turned into a stream which became almost a flood after the re-occupation of Singapore.

Before the implementation of the 10-year Medical Plan starting in 1950, which called for a chain of attractive child and maternity clinics to be built throughout rural Singapore, rural maternity and child welfare work was carried out in a great variety of quite unsuitable buildings, such as dilapidated shophouses, coolie lines, a police pound, an old chandu shop, the corner of a crowded shop or any place where there was shade and a table and a chair for the staff. Many areas could not be reached because of inadequate transport system in the rural areas. Still, much valuable work was done during this period, as reflected in the reduction of the rural infant mortality rate from

Home visits to provide pre-natal and post-natal care were made regularly by Health Nurses from the Maternal and Child Health Centres, c. 1960s.

One of the floating dispensaries usually carried a mobile maternity and child welfare team, consisting of a Lady Medical Officer and a nurse, who held antenatal and infant welfare clinics on the various islands, c. 1960s. Initially diffident and uncooperative, the islanders gradually came readily for treatment, and their health improved greatly.

c. 1950s.

c. 1950s.

187 in 1944 to 57 in 1948. The rural folks valued this work and in many instances, mothers travelled long distances with their children to attend the nearest clinic. There were also offers by the local population to collect funds to build up-to-date centres in their districts. For example; in 1949, the Rural District Committee of Bukit Panjang completed a new brick building for a modern welfare centre.

In 1951, a plan to re-organise the rural maternity and child welfare work on a regional basis was worked out:

I   There were to be seven regional centres staffed with nurses, midwives and health servants, anti-malarial overseers and hospital assistants. The latter were to run a static dispensary service also in each region.

II In addition, there were to be a number of residential maternity and child welfare centres with resident nurses and midwives only and these were to be supported by a series of subsidiary and clinic centres. The aim was to have some 100 centres of various kinds. It was hoped that as this part of the of the medical plan unfolded, each regional centre would eventually become a fully-equipped Rural Health Centre. These Rural Health Centres, in addition to providing facilities for maternity, child welfare and school medical work, would have a small laboratory, a dispensary and specialist services. As far as possible, these centres would work closely with community centres so that the latter's large auditorium and library facilities could be used for health education.

By the 1960s, there were seven large Rural Health Centres: at Nee Soon, Holland Road, Thomson Road, Serangoon Road, Yio Chu Kang, Ama Keng and Buona Vista. These were in addition to a network of major clinics , midwife stations and visiting centres throughout the rural and urban areas.

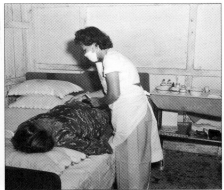
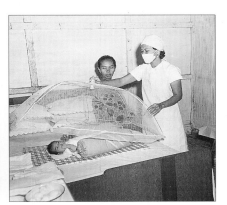

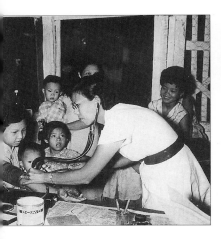

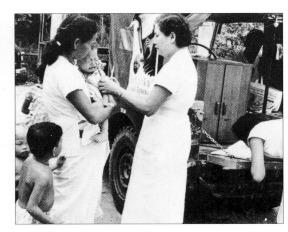

c. 1950s.   *c. 1950s.*

The Outpatient Service

The Outpatient Services began as a unit of the General Hospital manned by the hospital's doctors. In 1952, the services separated out as an independent department and the next year, moved into its own building in the hospital's grounds. It extended beyond the General Hospital with the establishment of satellite dispensaries throughout the island.

The Outpatient Service was essentially a general practitioner type of service. It was quite separate from the Outpatient Clinics run by the hospitals and hospital units, which were clinics where patients were followed up or where consultations were undertaken.

The following were grouped under the Outpatient Service:

I   The Outpatient Dispensaries

II   The Travelling Dispensaries

*Outdoor dispensary
in Jurong, c. 1960s.*

III   The Government-Staff Dispensaries

IV   The Institutional Hospitals ... The Prison Hospitals at Pearl's Hil and Changi Prison and the Opium Treatment Centre at St John's Island.

By the mid-1960s, there were 26 outpatient dispensaries in different parts of Singapore and two clinics in Pulau Ubin and Pulau Tekong.

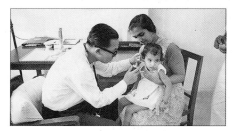

School Health

c. 1960s.

The School Health Service was started in 1921. The year before, a private practitioner was asked to undertake the medical examination of schoolchildren. He did this till 1921, when the nucleus of the present school services was born. The services expanded and from 1925 onwards, they were administered through the Government Health Department for all schools, both Municipal and Rural, until 1958, when it was centrally administered from the Institute of Health at Outram Road.

A school travelling dispensary was made available in March 1951 and placed under the charge of a health nurse, who visited rural schools situated away from school clinics for the treatment of minor ailments and to follow up cases referred by the School Health Officers. A second travelling dispensary was added a few years later.

As a start towards providing dental treatment for schoolchildren, a School Dental Clinic was established in 1948. Before

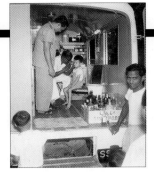

c. 1960s.

c. 1960s.

The Outpatient Services also operated travelling and floating dispensaries to meet minor medical needs of the people in the rural areas and the small islands off Singapore. The travelling units had different routes and visited fixed places at definite times each day. Boards indicating the regular stopping places where cases could be seen and treatment given were put up at strategic points. The units were under the charge of hospital assistants supervised by medical of-ficers. As rural areas lacked medical services available in the city, these travelling units served a real need and provided medical help in dealing with over 90 per cent of the rural dwellers' medical complaints.

In 1951, a floating dispensary was commissioned and launched to provide treatment, advice and health education to the small communities living off the main island. Another floating dispensary was launched in 1955.

c. 1960s.

c. 1960s.

this, the government only provided dental treatment through the dental clinic at the General Hospital, which was a joint treatment and teaching institution.

The first mobile dental clinic was placed on the road in March 1954. It was fully equipped and supplied with electricity from a generator towed on a trailer. The clinic housed a dental officer and a dental nurse who visited schools. A second mobile dental clinic came into service in 1956 and a third in 1957. The mobile clinics provided systematic treatment to rural schools.

1951.

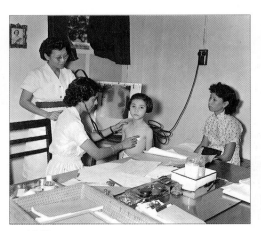

c. 1960s.

c. 1960s.

c. 1960s.

c. 1950s.

KAMPONG LIFE

Seen Through The Eyes Of A Working Adult

Preface

Fishermen setting off to sea in an evening of various hues and tones, farmers toiling amid a wash of lush greenery and the continual clucking of chickens … all romantic images by which we may like to remember rural life.

But in reality, life for the working adult in the village was a state of constant worry and hard work … families to take care of, bad weather which made fishing difficult, diseases which killed livestock, floods which destroyed crops, fires that left families homeless … leaving him little, if any, time for leisure…

Livelihood

A Pig Farmer

c. 1970s.

"We had a farm in Nam Ho Village in Lim Chu Kang in the 1950s. But then, the Lim Chu Kang area was different from what it is now," recollected Mr Ong Chau Ngak, whose family owned one of the largest pig farms in Singapore during the 1970s.

He elaborated: "The place where I was born used to be a swamp area and we built a dam from the soil and cleared the forest to start a farm. There were also many pythons and they were fond of chickens and ducks. One could easily find a python inside the house. Even when you sleep, the python could be just beside you."

According to Mr Ong, roads were muddy and at that time, Lim Chu Kang Road was the only tarred road.

In the late 1940s, Mr Ong's family grew mainly cucumbers and melons. But in the 1950s, they reared chickens, ducks and pigs on a small scale.

His family also owned 11 coconut farms in different parts of the village. He explained why the animal farms were also located at the coconut farms: "If you had planted coconut trees in one area, that area wouldn't be suitable for growing vegetables as the trees would block the sunlight. So you could only have animal farms at these places."

In the mid-60s, however, things changed for the Ongs.

The Primary Production Department

c. 1960s.

A peek into village life cannot be complete without a look at the Primary Production Department (PPD), which played, and still plays, an important role in the life of those involved in agriculture and fishing.

The PPD, which is responsible for the implementation of government policies on agricultural and fisheries development, came into being in 1960 and then comprised the Agriculture Division, Co-operative Development Division, Fisheries Division, Rural Development Division and Veterinary Division.

Today, the PPD, which is under the Ministry of National Development, consists of six divisions: Corporate Services, Agriculture, Agrotechnology, Fisheries, Veterinary and Veterinary Public Health.

Now, as previously, the PPD regulates farm activities, develops and manages farm

c. 1960s.

"*Our farm expanded after 1965 when there was a boom in business. By 1970 - 71, we had about 1,000 pigs in the farm. At that time, it was considered a large farm.*"

He added that by then, the farm operation was quite modern and machinery was used. "*We mixed the feed with a mixer and the amenities in the pig sties improved.*"

There was also competition among the farmers to produce the best livestock and dealers were willing to pay a high price if the meat was good.

"*But our pigs fetched higher prices than those of the other farms because our pigs were introduced from overseas. We also had many regular clients.*"

Mr Ong also said that they had a contract with one of their clients.

He said that the price of pork varied from day to day and that in the early 1970s, the selling price of about $60 - $70 per 100 kati was below cost, but that the price could sometimes increase to about $100 - $200.

"*Accumulation of pigs by dealers caused this change in prices. The dealers would stock up and then export them. But when Malaysia stopped importing pigs, there was an over-supply in Singapore. So, the dealers lowered the prices. We suffered losses then,*" he explained.

He added that the farm was bustling with activity all year round. "*We even worked on the first and second day of the Lunar New Year. There was never really any rest throughout the year.*"

c. 1970s.

Collection of Quek Tiong Swee, courtesy of National Archives.

c. 1970s.

Collection of Quek Tiong Swee, courtesy of National Archives.

estates, conducts research on intensive farm methods, animal husbandry and control and research on diseases, provides services to farmers and fishermen and identifies new sources of food supplies and facilitates their importation.

The PPD is now involved in a high-technology approach to farming as urbanisation continues to encroach on the cultivable lands of Singapore. Farmlands have been developed into agrotechnology parks which are provided with roads, utilities and other supporting services. Located at Sungei Tengah, Loyang, Muria, Lim Chu Kang, Jalan Kayu, Punggol and Pulau Ubin, these parks are used for livestock production, horticulture, freshwater fisheries, fruit orchards, marine fish and prawn farming and intensive vegetable cultivation.

c. 1960s.

c. 1960s.

A Fisherman

c. 1960s.

c. 1960s.

c. 1960s.

While most of us today may like to think of fishing as a relaxing hobby and entertain thoughts of a fisherman's life as being one of tranquility amidst the vast blue sea, fishermen in reality led lives that were contrary to all that we may imagine.

Bad weather at times endangered their lives or prevented them from going out to sea. There was little time for recreation, with most of their free time spent preparing for the next day's work, such as net mending, boat repairing or the doing of odd jobs to supplement the family's income.

On some of the hazards of being a fisherman, Mr Kahar bin Kurus recalled one stormy night when he went adrift: "The night was dark. I could not see the land. Then came the rain. The wind changed its direction. It was frightful. I felt like crying. At first I thought it was Ayer Gemuroh that I saw, but it was actually Padang Terbakar."

Mr Kahar, who had been a fisherman since 1929, added that most of his knowledge of the sea was gained from experience. He did not possess a compass nor did he know how to use one. He explained that a fisherman would not go further than two miles away from the beach.

Also, most fishermen could easily forecast the weather. "If the sky is dark without lightning, it is safe. But dark clouds with lightning here and there means that it will soon be raining," he explained.

He used the bubu (a form of fish trap) and fishing nets to catch fish. "I would normally go to the sea at night

if I wanted to use nets, not during the day, when fish can easily see the nets."

He said that it was easier to use fish traps than nets, except that he would have to remember where he had placed the traps.

Experience has taught him where to place the traps. "Fish are fond of gathering around corals and seaweeds. I can tell whether there are corals at the bottom because corals produce a bubbling sound. The traps would be left there for three days."

Mr Kahar earned about $70 - $80 per month before the Second World War, and about $300 per month after that. He said: "Much easier to sell my catch to a middleman than directly to the market. I could save time and money. Not many villagers came to buy as they were fishermen themselves."

But during the monsoon season, especially in December and January, most fishermen stayed ashore.

"Yet, between July and December, I would be able to get big fish though small in number. However, between March and June, the catch is bigger but the fish are smaller," he said.

So what do fishermen do during the monsoon?..Nothing...almost.

Mr Kahar, for one, spent time doing something profitable. He went around looking for people who needed haircuts, showing that his fisherman's hands could be nifty with the barber's tools as well.

c. 1960s.

c. 1960s.

c. 1960s.

A Poultry Farmer

c. 1960s.

c. 1960s.

c. 1970s.

Long hours and routine work! That was the life of a poultry farmer.

A normal day for the poultry farmer started around 6 am with the feeding of the chickens and checking of the water supply. The farmer inspected his farm for ailing birds and the conditions of the cages and sheds.

Round about noon, feedstuff was given to the chickens About three hours later, eggs were collected from the cages and sorted into paper trays in the house. As most farmers did not grade their eggs, sorting involved only the putting of the eggs in neat piles in the trays. Feed was again given after the collection of the eggs.

The farmer was busiest when the new batches of chicks were bought or when the birds fell sick or when a sale of poultry was being made. On the whole, farm work left the farmer with little leisure time and social outlets were few as farms were far apart and far from towns.

Although poultry rearing had always been fairly extensive in Singapore, both in the half-dozen or so "backyard fowls" raised for family use or in the larger numbers kept by Chinese squatter vegetable/pig rearers, poultry farming remained a sideline to a smallholder's farming till as late as 1947.

Perhaps one reason for this was the prevalence of the Ranikhet disease, which made poultry rearing too hazardous for it to be undertaken seriously. It was only after the introduction of the anti-Ranikhet vaccine produced at the Veterinary Research Laboratories at Ipoh that the activity expanded.

Mr Ong Chau Ngak, who had also reared poultry in his farm at Lim Chu Kang, recalled some of the hazards of poultry rearing. "We gave up chicken rearing because of one episode of epidemic which killed all the chickens. Therefore we weren't confident in the trade. We lost about 1,000 egg-laying birds whose breed was introduced from overseas. The loss incurred was enormous!"

As for the cause of the epidemic, he said: "Our birds received vaccinations regularly but that time they probably got it a little late. So, after the vaccination, all of them died."

He added that the epidemic could have been caused by a lack of environmental hygiene. "The virus could also have have travelled from another farm, say, if you take a walk in another farm and carry the virus back. When one of your birds gets the virus, all would be infected soon."

A Dairy Farmer

c. 1960s.

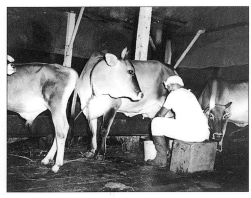

c. 1960s.

c. 1960s.

Work and life on a dairy farm revolved mainly around milking the cows, delivering the milk, cleaning the sheds, feeding the animals, cutting the grass and taking the animals out to graze.

Said Mr Muthu Sammy, who grew up on a dairy farm and later operated one at Jalan Somapah Timor: "We got up at about six in the morning and started with cleaning the shed. We started here first because there was cow dung everywhere. Then a man would come to milk the cows."

Mr Muthu, who did not milk the cows himself because of injuries following an accident, said that the man who did the milking used to own a farm too and was also one of his customers.

"This man had a lot of customers, so we thought that it would be easier for us to sell the milk to him and for him to deliver. We measured the milk in litres and he would pack them in bottles and sell them," added Mr Muthu, whose father had been rearing cows since the Japanese Occupation in 1942.

After the milking, the cows were fed with soya bean curd, wheat flour, wheat husk and sesame seed waste. These items had been bought and mixed into porridge.

After this, Mr Muthu would have breakfast before returning to clean the sheds.

"By the time they had eaten, the shed was dirty again, so we cleaned the place again," he said.

The cleaning would take him till noon, when it was feeding time again. In the afternoon, the cows would be milked and fed once more.

From about 4 pm to 6.30 pm, Mr Muthu would cut grass for animal feed. The cows would be fed with grass after the evening milking.

"By the time we fed them everything, it would be 7 or 7.30 pm already. Then we had a rest, then we had our shower, then had our dinner, then watched TV, and then went to bed. So the second day came, early morning wake up, got up again...At least I was kept busy. So really I was happy," said Mr Muthu in rounding off his account of the day's routine.

How does Mr Muthu view such a life?

"I didn't take a break. It was the same every day. Routine work. I am a simple man, I don't like to enjoy much. So, every day the same. Morning once you wake up you start to work. But I think that is good. It kept me healthy and you have more exercise. Move around. Do the work."

Vegetable Farming

c. 1960s.

c. 1960s.

c. 1960s.

In spite of the continuing shortage of cultivable land due to urbanisation and industrialisation, villagers have always considered the intensive growing of vegetables an important means of their livelihood.

In the mid-1950s, the most important vegetable-growing area was at the junction of Braddell Road and the Kallang River, where the land had been cultivated since the 1830s. The farmers there were almost all Cantonese and they used traditional methods with great success.

Generally, the Chinese method of cultivation is closely linked with pig rearing. Pigs are fed on discarded vegetables, sweet potato stems and water hyacinth. In return, the pigs provided all the manure needed for the vegetable plots. Sinks were erected near the pigsties and the manure allowed to rot until it became a turgid liquid which was then used to fertilise the vegetable plots. Where pig manure was not available, prawn dust was used and sometimes, human excreta was used too.

Another important vegetable-growing area was the Bedok Resettlement Area. The farmers there were mostly Hokkiens and Teochews but they used almost exactly the same methods as at Braddell Road.

Some other areas where leafy vegetables were planted:

a) Potong Pasir/Braddell Road

b) off Changi Road 9 1/2 m.s.

c) off Punggol Road 8 1/4 m. s.

Some areas where fruits and vegetables were planted:

a) off Yio Chu Kang Road 10 1/4 m. s.

b) off Sembawang Road 12 1/2 m. s.

c) off Marsiling Road 15 1/2 m. s.

In the mid-1960s, the pattern was to combine horticulture with foodcrop cultivation because of the increasing demand for land required for industrial development.

Monoculture was practised mainly in urban and suburban lowland areas like Potong Pasir and Changi where many kinds of leafy vegetables were planted and harvested in quick succession throughout the year for the local market.

Generally, the cultivation of leafy vegetables was concentrated in lowlands while fruits and root vegetables were grown in the more undulated areas.

But the Primary Production Department has projected that only 2,000 ha of such land would be left for farming in 1995.

A Shopkeeper

c. 1960s.

c. 1950s.

"At that time, most people bought things on credit. That was because they had to wait until they could sell their livestock or vegetables before they could get any money," recalled Mr Ong Ting Lye, who owned a provision shop in Mandai for about 50 years.

Mr Ong, 60, who lived in a village where most people were Teochew or Hokkien, added: "They usually had a book with them in which they would record the things they bought and would pay only about five or six months later. But of course I would see if he could be trusted first before I sold to him on credit."

Mr Ong's family used to own an orchard but they opened a provision shop on realising that they could make a better living by running a business.

"There was nothing elaborate about the shop. Just wooden shelves to put things on. And there was of course a safe to put money and valuables in. Most of the sundry goods were bought from Rochore Road while the rice was from either North Bridge Road or South Bridge Road," he said.

Customers then tended to shop around for the best prices more than they do now, he said. "Last time, people went to different shops to check out the prices and then bought from the cheapest shop, but now, it is different. The prices are about the same everywhere. But I did not necessarily sell my goods at the lowest price. It depended on how much I got them at. Some people bought them at a lower price, so they could afford to sell them at a lower price," he said.

He recalled how cheap some items were years ago. "Most things were cheap at the beginning but they got expensive as time went by. In the 1950s, one kati of rice cost about ten to twenty cents."

Mr Ong added that the location of a kedai or shop, even in a kampong, was important for good business. "My shop was at a place where people came to collect vegetables, so it was quite central and many people came to my shop. Moreover, I had a good relationship with my customers. You have to treat people well because one day, they could be your customers."

According to him, festivals like Chinese New Year or the Hungry Ghost Festival were the best time for business while the worst periods were from February to April, when there were no festivals.

And what of leisure time?

"I did not have much leisure time. When you worked from 6 am to 9 pm, you were too tired to do anything after that. And most of the villagers did not do much for leisure activities either. They were too tired after coming back from work in their farms."

Other Trades

Although most of us may think of farming and fishing as the main means of livelihood in the rural areas, villagers were also often engaged in many other economic activities, some of which are vanishing trades today.

An example of a village with varied economic activities is the kangkar at Nee Soon.

If you had walked around the kangkar in the mid-1980s, you would have found that the coffeeshop business was mainly monopolised by the Hainanese and the roti prata shops were managed by Indians. You would also have found a Chinese traditional confectionery established by a migrant from Fujian, spice shops owned by Indians, a laundry business managed by a Shanghainese, Chinese medicine shops established by the Hakkas and the like.

A similar example can be found in Geylang Serai, where villagers often found work outside their village. Some worked as hawkers, others as boatmen who towed traders into the harbour, yet others were basket weavers, medicine men, policemen, postmen or even members of musical groups.

Working on plantations was another common means of livelihood. Some of the early settlers in Jurong, for example, worked as rubber tappers or were casual labourers employed to weed grass.

Collection of The Straits Times Press, courtesy of National Archives.

c. 1960s.

c. 1960s.

c. 1900s.

c. 1970s.

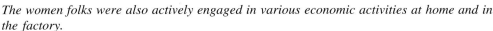

The women folks were also actively engaged in various economic activities at home and in the factory.

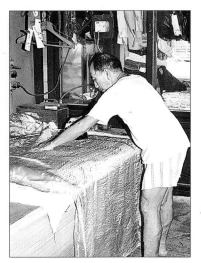

Although very much a vanishing trade now, the laundry business was one means of livelihood for people who lived in the rural areas, c 1970s.

Coconut plantations used to be a common sight in the outskirts of Singapore, c 1950s. Coconut husks were removed by spikes mounted on the grounds. The coconuts were sent to the refinery to manufacture coconut oil while the residue was fed to pigs. The coconuts were also sent to the market for sale.

The itinerant hawker was one of the sources from whom the villagers bought their daily necessities, c 1950s.

Communal Life

While taking care of their farms and jobs took up most of the time of the working adults in kampongs, some of them did find time to become members of the village community centres. One of them was Mr Ong Ting Lye.

"The government had its own network for finding out who were the good men. They were very strict in selection. You must have only one wife. You musn't have quarrelled with the other villagers. You must be a man of good character in order to be chosen," he said.

Elaborating, he said: "They would go round to the villagers and ask them about this man, whether this man was of negative or positive influence, and they would write a report and select those who were deemed suitable."

He said the activities of the Community Centre (CC) included the provision of electricity, lamp posts and other amenities. The CC also ran a kindergarten and screened movies.

"There were graduation ceremonies at the kindergartens and every two years, there would be a celebration for the anniversary of the CC and there would be all sorts of recreational activities like basketball tournaments," he recalled.

In the beginning, the villagers shied away from such activities, but they later became more supportive.

"When the CC started, with the conducting of classes like dressmaking and cookery, the

The rural CC was usually a one-storey building made largely of plank and zinc, in an open area and villagers were relatively free to come into the centre's compound at any time of the day. Although spartan, the CC was nonetheless functional and catered adequately to the needs of the rural population, c. 1960s.

Convinced that mass mobilisation and mass support were essential for community and national development, the People's Action Party Government set about creating grassroots organisations after winning the 1959 general elections. The People's Association was established on July 1, 1960. Within six months, it built 18 CCs to encourage cultural and recreational activities. For the first time, from the 1960s onwards, villagers had proper recreational facilities like exercise rooms, table-tennis and billiards tables, and basketball and badminton courts. There were also sewing, cookery and handicraft classes for young ladies and housewives, and joget and dancing lessons for everyone.

c. 1960s.

c. 1960s.

c. 1960s.

c. 1960s.

villagers began to feel that the CC was bringing a positive contribution to the village so they became more positive. Serving on the CC not only meant time and energy but also a lot of money. The chairman usually set an example and he would make a certain donation, then the vice-chairman...it went down the line. It was a lot of effort and time — they held meetings every month and also there was a lot of money contributed to the CCs."

Mr Ong said of his role in the CC: "The CC did have its full-time staff. They had a secretary or an assistant there. My role was like, if there was a function, then I would assist or provide feedback about policies that affected the village. If, say, there was a quarrel or dispute, I would bring it to the secretary. Usually, they would try and resolve the dispute by consulting me as the mediator. They would not take it to court or make it a big issue."

He said that the issues then included the supply of water and electricity, street lamps and roads.

"What I did if the villagers wanted these was to draw up a map and proposal to present to the MP. The MP would then present to the ministry. So that was basically what we did."

Mandai Village C C, c. 1960s.

Opening of Tuas C C by Mr Chor Yeok Eng, Assemblyman for Jurong, 1960.

c. 1960s.

c. 1960s.

Leisure

In the early days, the villagers had few entertainment facilities. During the 1950s and 1960s, the Public Relations Office and subsequently the Ministry of Culture provided film shows, such as documentaries, for the villagers. The turnout at these shows was always overwhelming.

Sometimes, the film teams also gave brief talks on current topics nightly to audiences at the film shows, c. 1950s. At other times, they dramatised announcements.

Village cinemas provided cheap entertainment for kampong folks, c. 1960s. The average charges were about 50 cents for adults and 30 cents for children. The cinemas showed mostly Chinese films and patrons were mainly local kampong people and those from the neighbouring kampongs.

Opera shows, staged during festivals and religious celebrations, were another common form of entertainment, c. 1960s.

With the coming of television in the mid-1960s, the villagers either went to watch the televised programmes at the CC or else, if they could afford, installed their own television sets at home. Open-air cinemas and opera shows started to lose their popularity.

Caught up in the world of make-believe at a story-telling session, the cares of this world are temporarily forgotten, c. 1950s.

Two residents having a game of chess in Kampong Siglap, 1980.

A relaxing stroll or swim by the beach with its swaying trees, golden sand and blue sea cost kampong folks nothing, c. 1950s.

A mobile library service point at Kaki Bukit Community Centre, 1967. The National Library started its mobile library service to the rural areas around the mid-1960s. Between 1964 and 1967, weekly services of up to two hours, usually in the evenings, were provided at various points, but mainly the CCs, in areas like the West Coast (1964), Nee Soon (1965), Bukit Panjang (1966), Chong Pang/Kaki Bukit/Kampong Tengah/Bukit Timah/Changi 10 m. s./ Paya Lebar (1967). The service introduced many kampong folk, particularly the children, to the joys of reading.

The idyllic kampong landscape provided the perfect setting for family members to relax and enjoy each other's company, 1953.

Better roads meant heavier traffic for most villages, as in this kampong in Upper Serangoon Road, c. 1970s.

c. 1960s.

DEVELOPMENT AND RESETTLEMENT

Preface

Although rural life was romantic and rustic, it also meant that kampongs were cut off from the outside world, with no means of external communication.

In the 1950s, 1960s, and even up to the 1970s, a series of public works such as postal and police services, road reconstruction and repairs and flood alleviation schemes were systematically undertaken in the rural areas by the government to improve the villagers' standard of living.

Gradually, at about the same time, the government began its resettlement programme for the rural areas. In quite a few cases, kampong dwellers were rehoused in Housing Board flats after their homes were devastated by fire or flood. In most cases, however, villagers were resettled as their rustic dwellings were cleared for urban redevelopment.

While nostalgia and sadness at having to leave familiar surroundings were apparent in residents at times, most of them understood that the old must give way to the new for progress and accepted the challenge to build new homes for themselves and to adapt to what the future might hold...

POSTAL And
POLICE FACILITIES

In the early days, not every village had a post office. Gradually, a network of mobile post offices, sub-post offices, postal agencies and post boxes emerged to provide better postal facilities for rural people.

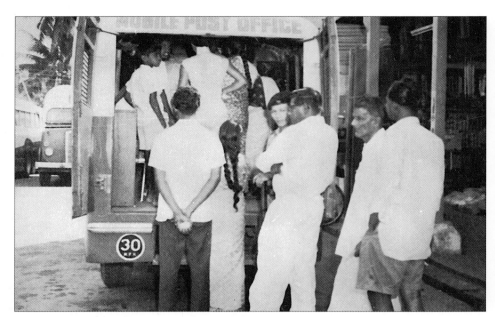

The Mobile Post Office was introduced in 1952 to provide postal facilities in the rural areas where there were no post offices. The van ran to a schedule and stopped at the same place and time one day each week. A second van was placed in service in 1955.

Postal agency at Tuas Village, 1960.

Postal delivery to the rural areas, on foot or bicycle, continued despite rain and flood, 1956.

A constable on kampong patrol, like the one in this 1962 picture, toured every kampong in the rural areas. He was a familiar figure with the villagers and was always welcomed wherever he went as he offered advice and assistance to all rural dwellers.

A village constable talking to a Malay fisherman on the west coast of Singapore, 1953.

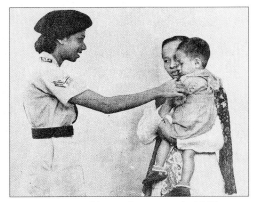

Woman constable on foot patrol, 1950. Women police were enrolled for the first time in March 1949.

Police Week at the Pasir Panjang Police Station, 1958. The first Police Week was organised in 1958 to foster good police-public relations. During the Week, 370,000 people, nearly a quarter of the population, visited 12 main police establishments which were open to the public each evening. Police stations were crammed with men, women and children of all communities, studying posters, inspecting lock-ups and listening to talks and appeals for co-operation. Each station was decorated and floodlit, and the officers and men themselves acted as guides and hosts. The next Police Week was held in June 1971, 13 years later.

Road Development and Transport

Zion Road c. 1950s.

Except for an occasional access road leading into it, there were usually not many main roads in the rural areas. The earliest roads in kampongs were probably dirt tracks and gravel roads. Most of these were narrow and in need of complete reconstruction, realignment and widening.

Road development on a larger scale took place after the establishment of the Rural Board in 1909.

In the 1950s, the most common form of road construction consisted of a wearing course of pre-mixed asphalt, a binder course of pre-coated stone or penetration macadam and base courses of waterbound macadam carried on a sub-base or quarry waste. The PWD later replaced roads built this way, first with rubber roads and then with concrete roads.

But kampong roads remained more or

Mr R. A. Gonzales, Member of Parliament for Serangoon Gardens, and a team of 300 people repairing Cheng San Road, badly damaged by a flood in 1967.

Mr Yong Nyuk Lin and University of Malaya students repairing a road at Lorong 23, Geylang, in 1961.

The bullock cart, the earliest mode of transportation, was used for both people and goods, c 1900s.

The most popular modes of transportation in the early 1900s were the bullock cart and the rickshaw. The bicycle also came in handy for getting around the kampong. It was their feet, however, that most kampong folk relied on for taking them everywhere.

The setting up of the Singapore Electric Tramways in 1902 brought limited change to the transportation scene in the

rural areas. The only two areas to enjoy the services of the tramway were Geylang and Serangoon roads. The Singapore Traction Company (STC) was set up in 1925. The Trolley Bus System covered 25 miles of route and, with 108 vehicles, claimed to be the largest trolley bus network in the world. But there were not enough trolley buses to cover all the residential areas and buses

Later, the rickshaw was a godsend for kampong folks who found the walk from the bus stop to the kampong too long but could not afford a bicycle, 1920.

Taxi services have been available since pre-war days but they were used mainly by British military personnel and their families who could afford them. Taxi stands like this one in Nee Soon, c. 1970s, were built by the Rural Board.

less bumpy till the late 1960s, when resettlement led to the widening and reconstruction of roads.

Mrs Ellamah Govindasamy, a housewife who lived in the Naval Base in Sembawang, recalled: "Roads were very well maintained within the Naval Base area but Sembawang Road was still not really cleared until after the Second World War. It always flood whenever it rained. After 1969, the road was widened and it was made into a dual carriageway and drainage works were carried out."

The early 1960s saw a shortage of construction workers and it was quite common for villagers to get together to clean up or even build roads. At times, other people were roped in to help as well. This spirit of community help or "gotong royong" was common in kampongs and helped not only to unite the people but also to teach them the value of hard work.

Opening of Coronation Road (West) by Acting Chief Minister Enche Jumat, 1957.

Villagers of Nee Soon, including students and national servicemen, embarking on road building campaigns in the 1960s and 1970s.

The completion of a new road was a joyous and grand affair. The entire kampong turned up to watch the event, complete with lion dances, ribbon-cutting ceremony and a small reception.

were introduced from London to make up for the shortage. Of 16.5 miles served by the buses, 10.5 miles were in the rural districts.

To improve rural transportation, the Municipal Council allowed the running of "mosquito buses". These were eight-seater buses run by independent Chinese companies At bus stations, they would squeeze in as many passengers as possible and dash off at breakneck speed. Other private operators worked along the rural roads linking the kampongs and bringing passengers to the nearest trolley bus terminals from which they could continue their journey into town on another vehicle. An estimated eleven Chinese bus companies were in operation in 1954, and each plied in and around a particular rural area.

During the war years, the STC had a "business hours only" service to the village in Bukit Timah. After the war, pirate taxis operating like mosquito buses were seen everywhere. It was also common to see motorcycles and cars whizzing around the kampongs.

A typical Easy Austin Bus Company's "Austin", seen here with the STC buses at the Tampines Terminus, 1956. Service 3 was a popular service which ran across town from the General Hospital, crossed the Kallang River and travelled on to the junction of Geyland Road and Grove Road, which was renamed Mountbatten Road after the Second World War.

The bicycle was an important mode of transport in the village, c, 1960s. Bicycles were especially important to villagers living in remote areas who sometimes had to travel 5-6 km to reach the main road.

c. 1960s.

Grim reality for farmers...carcasses of pigs seen after a flood, c. 1950s.

Collection of Lianhe Zaobao, courtesy of National Archives.

Providing relief for flood victims, 1958.

Like fire victims, flood victims often lost their identification documents and were sometimes made homeless. They too had to join long queues to register for new documents or apply for new homes, 1958.

SINGAPORE, Saturday.
POLICE were put on stand-by alert today after continuous rain since last night flooded 28 areas in the Republic.

Collection of Lianhe Zaobao, courtesy of National Archives.

When the floods came, the only means of transportation was often the sampan or some other small boat. Vehicles were useless until the floodwaters had subsided, c.1950s.

When it rained heavily during the monsoon season, villagers had one great fear: flood.

Unlike today's Singapore, which has a sophisticated and well-planned drainage systems to prevent heavy flooding and where most people live in flats which are less prone to flood damage, the Singapore of the 1950s and early 1960s was less fortunate, particularly for those who lived in kampong houses.

The Joint Committee on Flood Alleviation was formed in 1951 to tackle the common rural problem of flooding, by improving drainage.

Floods had a devastating effect on those in the rural areas. Besides drowning people and animals, floods also caused landslides, and uprooted trees and other structures. In 1969, a landslide buried an attap hut occupied by a sleeping family and, despite rescue efforts, a woman and her son were killed. In another incident, a man was crushed to death by a falling coconut tree.

Those who depended on the land for their livelihood were also affected by floods. In October 1954, a two-day flood caused considerable damage to the Bedok Resettlement Area. Even more widespread floods in December that year resulted in great losses of livestock around the Geylang Serai - Lorong Tai Seng area and losses to vegetable farmers in the Potong Pasir and Braddell Road area.

An estimated loss of $247,000 for about 910 farms, or $271 per farm, was suffered during this flood.

About 2,500 inhabitants of Bedok Resettlement Area were made homeless by floods in February 1954. Thousands of dollars worth of livestock, fodder and household property were destroyed as water levels in the area rose to nearly 6 ft. In all, about 5,000 people, mostly from the rural areas, were made homeless by the flood.

"During the floods in 1967 and 1968, the water reached to about four to five feet high. It rained very heavily and the sea water broke the dam. We could not take any preventive measures for the water came very suddenly. We could only hope that the water would not get any higher," said Mr Ong Chau Ngak about his experiences with floods at his village.

He was more fortunate than the farmers in Bedok in the 1950s though, as his farm buildings were on high ground and were not flooded.

"Besides, the pigs were clever enough to secure their front legs to the railings of the pigsty so as to keep their heads above water and they had to stay in that position for three hours until the water lowered!" he added in recalling how his farm survived the flood.

He also remembered that the other farms were not affected because they too occupied higher ground.

OCEAN
MOTOR POLICIES

The Straits Times Press

THE OCEAN
ACCIDENT AND GUARANTEE
CORPORATION, LTD.
(Incorporated in Great Britain)
Head Office for Malaya: SINGAPORE

20 PAGES.   SINGAPORE, THURSDAY, AUGUST 9, 1934.   PRICE 10 CENTS.

Scenes of Desolation In Singapore

THE SCENES OF DESOLATION at Tiong Bahru, Bukit Ho Swee and Havelock Road. 1. All that is left of what was a populous area yesterday. 2. Hoses playing on the smouldering ruins. 3. It is estimated that 39,000 feet of hose-pipe was called into use by the fire brigade. 4. Many trees shared the fate of the dwellings. 5. Searching for any property which may have escaped destruction. 6. A picture that speaks for itself.

Printed and Published by Edward Gill at the Straits Times Press, Ltd., (Incorporated in the Straits Settlements) Cecil and Stanley Streets, Singapore, Straits Settlements.

Houses made of wooden planks and attap roofs burnt too readily. Strong winds made it possible for entire villages to be destroyed in a matter of a few hours. These made the villagers susceptible to another hazard: fire.

The causes for fires were varied. They ranged from an overturned kerosene stove to burning joss paper and firecrackers The Straits Times of 3 February 1968 reported that firecrackers were believed to be responsible for 62 fires during a single week. But in many cases, the causes were not known.

Three outbreaks of fire which remain fresh in the minds of people of the older generation are the ones in 1934, 1961 and 1968 in Bukit Ho Swee.

In the 1934 fire, three kampongs in Tiong Bahru, Bukit Ho Swee and Havelock Road were destroyed. The homes of over 500 families went up in the blaze and about 5,000 were made homeless.

Because of a lack of any authority to control or check the housing situation, squatter huts similar to those destroyed again sprang up there.

The 1961 blaze started at a hillside squatter district in Kampong Tiong Bahru near the site of an earlier fire in 1959. The fire spread rapidly through an attap colony till it reached Tiong Bahru itself. Strong winds fanned the fire through the kampong right up to Havelock Road. Several blocks

of SIT flats, hundreds of attap huts, oil mills, timber yards and motor shops were destroyed.

"I was at home with my brother washing, cutting and shaving sweet potatoes when the fire broke out," recalled Madam Tung of the 1961 fire at Bukit Ho Swee.

"Suddenly, I thought I heard someone shout 'Fire!'. I told my brother and then I dragged him out of the house to wait for my mother. Just then, my mother came home and threw her basket and took us to the pond nearby. Then she went back into the house to grab some pillows and blankets and went back to the pond."

An area of about 60 acres extending from the southern side of Tiong Bahru Road to the northern side of Havelock Road was devastated and about 16,000 people made homeless by the fire.

After the 1961 fire, immediate rehousing of most of the fire victims in Housing Board flats was arranged. Newly-completed flats in Queenstown, St Michael Estate, MacPherson Road and Kallang Airport were made available for occupation.

The Housing Board was also instructed by the government to prepare for the development of the fire site and to reclaim about 150 acres of the surrounding area. Plans were drawn up for the building of 12,000 units of flats and shops on the site. By the end of the next year, 3,228 units of flats were completed at the fire site with another 2,000 units still under construction.

Scenes at the 1961 Bukit Ho Swee fire. The scenario was to repeat itself in 1968.

On 9 March 1963, a fire razed Kampong Ban Kee (near Havelock Road) to the ground and made 3,000 people homeless. The fire was believed to have started after a kerosene stove overturned in the kitchen of an attap hut.

Most of the fire victims were housed at the Park Road School, 1963. During the first night of the ordeal, they were served a cup of hot coffee and biscuits and later given a meal.

The Kampong Ban Kee fire victims were housed in new flats at Bukit Ho Swee and Upper Pickering Street, 1963.

Although life in the kampong was blissful for some, it cannot be denied that many people were living under inadequate housing conditions with poor sanitary conditions, few social, recreational and other amenities, and the threats of fire and flood. It was only a matter of time before those living in the kampongs would be resettled in flats and housing estates which are found all over Singapore today.

Kampong folks moving to high - rise living in HDB flats, 1963.

New Homes For Old

Cramped and unsanitary living conditions in the rural areas, c.1960s.

As early as 1927, the Singapore Improvement Trust (SIT) was formed to improve housing conditions in Singapore. However, the problem was not solved because the SIT lacked the legal authority and financial support from the government for its building programmes.

In the 1960s, the present government made public housing programmes one of the top priorities of national development. Large-scale high-rise public housing programmes were carried out to solve the acute overcrowding and housing problems. This was also a phase of a massive resettlement programme.

The first five-year building programme started in 1961. It was projected by the government that 15,000 units would be needed between 1961 and 1970. By the end of 1970, a total of 120,669 units exceeding the target of the two five-year building programmes by 10,000 units.

In the first 10 years, from 1960 to 1969, a total of 37,000 squatters were cleared and paid $29 million in compensation. More people were resettled and more resettlement compensation awarded in the years that followed. From 1970 to 1979, more than 14,000 squatters were resettled with payments totalling $305 million while from 1980 to 1983, another 60,512 squatters were resettled and paid $505.4 million in compensation. In 1983, the HDB announced its plans to clear the backlog of 60,000 resettlement cases by

HDB flats in Queenstown, c. 1960s.

Interior views of a flat, c. 1960s.

the end of 1989.

Compensation rates were: $26.90 for squatter huts; $20 to $40 for fruit trees such as coconuts, durians and rambutans; and $741 per hectare of vegetable beds.

Families affected by clearance received compensation of $450 (sub-tenant) and $600 (house owner) to help them relocate to their new homes. They were also given a rental subsidy of $15 per month for three years. Shopkeepers who were relocated to Housing Board shops were given a five-year subsidy of 50 per cent of the shop rental for the first year, 40 per cent for the second year, 30 per cent for the third year, 20 per cent for the fourth year and 10 per cent for the fifth year.

Despite these compensations, some of those resettled found difficulty in adjusting to their new lifestyle.

Recalled Mr Ong Ting Lye: "It was very hard for those villagers who were farmers in their 40s or 50s to find a job in the factories. It was difficult for their skills were not applicable for the factories. Also, for some of the villagers, it was quite a major change of lifestyle, some of them had their livestock while others had crops. They were self-sufficient. But if they moved to flats, they had to buy everything and pay for everything."

Yet, on the whole, most of those resettled took to their new lifestyle. A survey by the HDB revealed that more than half of them reported that life had become better while only about 11 per cent said that life had become worse.

Said Madam Tung: "The flat was much cleaner, no snakes or mice, and more hygienic, we had our own taps so there was no need to fetch water for every trivial chore like cooking or washing nor was there need to queue up or rush with crowds. Also, for some, the flat was much bigger than the kampong house. The kampong house was lined in a long stretch made up of tiny rooms with many people living inside."

But though many facilities came with life in an HDB flat, for those who had spent their childhood and a large part of their adult life in the kampong, the nostalgia for kampong days never really dies.

Said Madam Poh: "In the kampong everyone knew each other. There was no need to shut your doors the whole day. If a stranger came to the kampong, we would inform each other and strangers rarely came in the night. I wish I could travel back in time and return to the kampong lifestyle."

Landscaped surroundings and modern amenities are found in most housing estates, c. 1980s.

c. 1950s.